FALLING OFF THE ROOF

Karen Lindsey

Library of Congress number 75-21788
ISBN: 0-914086-08-1
Printed in the United States of America

cover drawing, "Pandora's Box", by Emily Culpepper

Many of these poems have appeared in
The Second Wave; others have appeared in
*Everywoman, Hanging Loose, Haiku Highlights,
Sanskaris, Womanpoems, The Common Woman,
The Speculum,* and *The Smith.*

The publication of this book was supported by a
grant from the Massachusetts Council on the Arts and
Humanities.

Second printing.

Alice James Books are published by Alice James
Poetry Cooperative, Inc.

ALICEJAMESBOOKS
138 Mount Auburn Street, Cambridge, Massachusetts 02138

*for Dr. Viola Krider
and Dr. Steven Stepanchev,*

*who taught me how to write
poetry and how to survive*

"I want a women's revolution like a lover.
I lust for it. . . ."

Robin Morgan, MONSTER

CONTENTS

To a Male Poet who Told Me I was Talented but Wrote too
Much Like a Woman

STRATEGIES

**to a male poet who told me i was "talented,
but wrote too much like a woman"**

you still havent realized it, have you?
you still dont know your
definitions are dead.
we killed them with laughter, and rusty chains;
we left them dead under desert suns.
didnt you understand?
didnt you notice their bones crumbling into chalk,
scattering in frail breezes?
we have our own words now:
they are born of our breasts,
of the blood trickling down our legs.
they are born of the slow thickening of our waists,
of our barrenness,
of our frigidity, of our orgasms.
they are born of our lusts, of our indifference, of our lovers and our love
they are not born of you, they are not sired by you.
they are not even inspired by you, we will not
dedicate them to you, with gratitude.
they are ours, they are us,
and they will not go away again.

WOMEN AND OTHER LOVES

for sandra

i

they try to make death smell like flowers,
and they make flowers smell like death.
it's called a viewing, for my friend's father.
there are no windows, but the room's cold. the room's
cold.
i come to give you what i can,
and i wait, watching the flowers
in their bright, almost gaudy impotence.
my impotence i
cloak in a dark dress,
hugging a dark corner,
waiting, thinking of what i can give you.

ii

once i saw a photo of a man and woman on the shore
and a white blotch on the ocean.
the caption said the man and woman "watch helplessly
as their baby is carried off by the sea."
it's always like that.
your hand's transparent to my touch.

iii

the air's cold.
you don't cry; what i say is only the comfort of sound.
what i would give you, if i could.

iv

when i leave, the air is
warm from exhaust fumes and dirt. and it's lovely.
i want to run in two directions.
so i walk away slowly.
as if it were
a compensation.

vegetarian

flesh over bone
skin over flesh
hair.
the setting of eyes
equalizing of breasts
shaping of legs.
and always there is the waiting
for some great jaw to snap shut,
undo the whole thing.
it takes so long to grow a body
so much pain
so much ridicule if the job's done wrong.
flesh is meant to die; death
is necessary, perhaps even good.
but it is not my job.
i hide my body from the hungry jaws,
and hunt the hills for caves and camouflage
for myself, and all my friends.

fishing poem

out on the bay,
the rowboat, anchored, floats toward a brown house on shore.

my father is fishing.
                    a flounder
flaps in the pail,
his mouth gone: they pulled the hook out
quickly, so he wouldnt eat the worm (who's
dead now; before, he
wriggled on the hook a lot; i don't think he wanted to die
                                        just yet—)

i love my father.
i hope he catches a swordfish and it stabs him.
i sit on the boat, facing
the sea, facing the shore.
i'm pretending.
that the boat is moving, heading
toward the brown house.

that there's one fish, & I'm very brave, and I take it away from
my father, very gently, & say,
i'm sorry, fish, & start to throw it back only it
becomes a
sea-prince, who takes my hand & says, lets go,
so we do—down, down into a golden
seaworld, a castle made of
foam, & beautiful mermaids & lots of
dope & fucking & every
day when daddy goes fishing we go up & warn the
fish & put beer cans & old condoms on
daddy's line, & giggle

daddy its cold on this
boat & that house is no
closer than it was an hour ago.
i wish we could go home.

i wish that crab would bite you before you kill him.

i wish you'd stop fishing and cry a little.

for larry

trapped, the animal
    gnaws off its dying limb
choosing pain over slow death
    severing self from self.

you will be luckier.
the mind, gnawed free,
grows its own limbs.

elegy for sadmother—february 1975

Fur gray-white and shabby,
body squat, head too large—
he spent the daytime on our sunlit porch,
and greeted me with the morning mail.
Long since abandoned,
he had lived for years on his wits
and the kindnesses of neighbors.
Through so many seasons he had survived this way,
we never questioned his endurance:
he died in this year's cold.

Sadmother, you were a decent friend.
Your absence greets me daily.

jo ann

knowing it is useful to have a hobby,
you have become a weaver of rainbows.
you collect old clouds,
bits of sea-foam clinging to wet sand,
wisps of fur that fall into your hand
when you caress a passing kitten.
gently, you scrape the scabs of tears
from the faces of sleeping friends.
at night you weave them into rainbows,
to be used as gifts for christmases and weddings,
and amulets against madness.
when you prick your fingers
blood flows into the rainbows,
and smiles, and thoughts, and terrors.

men do not believe you are a rainbow weaver,
because you say words like cocksucker,
and once tried out
for the college football team.

MYTHS AND GAMES,
FANTASIES AND FANCIES

"We must break through the old roles
to encounter our own meanings in the
symbols we experience . . . What we use we must remake."—Marge Piercy

two haiku

winter... on the ocean,
the sun
shivers

dreary morning...
the empty mailbox
yawns

rain poem

thunder crawls across the dingy-pearl sky/

in a small puddle
circles of rain
blend into, out of
each other
like court dancers centuries gone

always, here, the dances mingle
of other worlds and times/
scottish mary laughing in her french palace
druids, elves
animal-women hunched over newfound flame

the arched foot poised over unknown planets

merged in the merging waters of the rain

poem reluctantly written at quarter of four
in the morning

if el greco had known me
he would have given me the view of toledo.
say he'd been handsome, and we were lovers.
or pals, anyway, moving in the same crowds.
if you like it so much, he'd have said, take it.
i, of course, moon-eyed, refusing,
finally accepting—
and long after we'd lost touch,
i'd have it, on a wall in a little, dark room
all my own
and all the time looking, looking at it
till a day came
when the dark, raincloud road turning off the right
would slither from the picture,
trail down to the floor,
smooth itself under my feet
and off, off i'd go,
soft, into toledo
and nothing changed in the picture,
no new figure, tiny on the road,
no face looking from a hidden graywhite window
back
on an old, gone world

flights

i

earthbound. steelbound.
there is no flight
in the cold precision of planes.
they move
from one spot to another, charted,
predictable as coloring books.
they are made of no magic.

ii

leave the plane,
slide into the cloud.
it is made of velvet, and the footsteps of spiders.
she is not surprised to see you; nothing
has surprised her since the day she came here.
she smiles, and teaches you to walk clouds.
she teaches you to touch rainbows,
and your hand becomes sea-moss,
the yellow silence before rain.
she has lived here
longer than your dreams of her.
she has discovered silence, and woven the sunset into her smile.

iii

you do not return,
and no one misses you.

five fantasies on a pair of sour-faced mannequins: bride and bridesmaid

first fantasy
they are really very happy but
the rehearsal has gone on all day and the
flower girl just sprained her ankle.

second fantasy
they were lovers but the
bride left her because
the groom had money and because someone said,
women dont do that with other women.

third fantasy
she is angry because
weddings are stupid and the gown was
sixty-seven dollars and ugly and the bride's family should have paid for it.

fourth fantasy
it is a masquerade and they have come
as their own most ludicrous memory:
in this fantasy, they are also lovers.

fifth fantasy
it is the happiest day of their lives.

allergy

its cold in your house but
i dont mind, its a
lovely visit & i enjoy your
apricot wine.
until i sneeze; you
apologize & turn up the heat.
im sorry, you say, we've gotten used
to low temperatures here.
oh no, i say, its just my allergy.
i look for my blue pills & cant find them.
i drink some apricot wine. i
sneeze.
you turn up the heat.
no really, i say. really its not that.
you smile, i take off my sweater.
my nose tickles, i try to stop it, i
sneeze, you turn up the heat.
your face is blue water, it ripples into a smile.
you dont understand, i say, sneezing again.
the heat goes up. my eyes water, its a hundred degrees,
your plastic flowers wilt. i
touch them. red wax coats my finger.
i sneeze, take off my clothes.
its snowing out, you say, listen to that wind.
you reach for the thermostat. i try to
protest, my throats too dry. i sneeze four times.
the floors steam.
ice cubes clink in your glass.
isnt this cozy? you ask.
i try to open a window; it sticks. my skin
puckers like an apricot. dries up.
flakes of it fall to the floor.
does the cold always affect you this way? you ask.
i sneeze, i run to the door, its locked.
my eyes run, tears scab my face.
its been a very cold winter, you say,
& put on my sweater.

the possibilities of nothing

the possibilities of nothing are
greater than you have known;
they are eyeless monsters,
blood brothers of the sun;
they do not eat,
still, they will tear apart your skin
to use your bones for toothpicks.
you say of an old time: it was not enough.
it was hunger fed on stale candy bars,
it was not enough.
as if there could be enough
as if enough were a place on a map
followed by lines of red arrows.
you say, it was next to nothing.
there is nothing next to nothing,
even despair covers the mind like warm flannel.
the possibilities of nothing are everywhere,
they swell the earth, they are the earth's children.
they steal your face and sell it for scrap metal,
they erase your name
and leave you no desert to wander in;
they use your blood to paint their faces,
and they have no faces.
you treat them lightly, you call other things by their names;
you have not watched them treading through the night
gouging out stars like old men's eyes.

the house on baltic avenue

first i buy baltic avenue from my friend,
for a railroad and fifty dollars.
(my friend says, women make lousy capitalists.)
then i buy a dreary little house, put it on baltic avenue,
and give it rent-free to a little old lady with seventy-eight cats,
who had to move from her old apartment.
it was getting too cramped there, she says, the cats werent happy.
i have a friend with ninety-four cats, she says,
but thats a little too much, dont you agree?
i agree.
the cats all have names, of course, & the little old lady
uses every letter in the alphabet at least once.
theres a cat named xerxes, and one named quarantine.
xerxes is my favorite. she rubs against my leg, cries to be petted.
i hold her in my lap, rub my face in her soft silver hair.
purring, she cleans my hand. the old lady smiles, and offers me tea.
when someone lands on my property, i take the money and buy catfood
big bags of it. pour it into seventy-eight yellow bowls, listen to their teeth
crunching, crunching. xerxes looks up, thanks me, resumes her eating.
rapunzel finishes, licks her face clean, twitches her ear,
wraps her tail around herself.
well, so long for now, i say.
goodbye, says the old lady.
& im bankrupt. out of the game.
the house gone.
i go back to baltic avenue, looking for the old lady and her cats.
nowhere. no trace, no forwarding address.
the neighbors say, she was upset about the house.
maybe she hanged herself on the clothesline in the back, they say.
i dont know about that.
they tell me the cats are all gone, scattered.
there are rumors that they've joined forces with the rats,
and are gnawing through the pipes at the water company.
i hope so.
i think maybe its true.
my friends go on playing.
i smile, sit back,
wait for the flood.

queens

when i play chess
i sacrifice the king to save the queen.
my friend smiles and says, you can't do that.
when i play chess
i lose the bishop to save the knight.
i do not allow horses to die for the games of men.
my friend says, that's not the way to play.
i smile.
he's getting mad.
when i play chess
i sacrifice the castles to save the pawns,
though castles are prettier.
my friend says, it isn't done that way.
i know, i say, but it's my game now.
i mean, the board's mine, this time.
your move, i say.
i can't play this way, he says.
the queen wins the game.

solitaire

sorrow of the faces
red jack on black queen, weeping
no drying, no drying
the lost tears of black-ink eyes
        the numbers are neutral.
calming, the dark 3's, one by one, simple
patterns of red 4's
calming, while birds scream in dead gray air
black 5 on red 6
red ace, building of diamonds,
wings flapping, gray air oozing
while fingers turn
a card, learn the
rectangles' slight mystery
        hush, the birds are flapping
the tiny vultures have found their corpses, and the streets
                    are dying
hush, there's no joker, the sick laughter's lost
and blood is only the red of diamonds and hearts, motion
of fingers on rectangles,
win the game? or lose and play again? or win and play again?
and the flappings grow louder
but still, still,
        to the sorrows of dark kings, what to say?

18

vampire

when they found they'd given birth to a vampire
they had her eye teeth removed.
it was a delicate operation;
still, they said, it was worth it.
for her fifth birthday, they bought her a yellow dress.
she got a nosebleed all over it, and laughed.
they got scared.
when she started her period,
they bought her boxes of white things that promised
not to impair her virginity, and told her not to be frightened.
she wasnt.
it's my blood, she said, i know what to do with it.
in school, the nuns prayed for her, every day.
one nun had a tiny phial, with the
blood of a holy martyr in it.
they found it one day under a desk, empty.
no one said anything, but her parents
sent her to the dentist to see if the teeth had grown back.
she bit his hand, and licked her lips.
next day she stole a suitcase and left town.
still, they all know she's there,
and no one goes out after dark.
they tuck their daughters into bed, and lock the doors.
they say, we should have killed her back then,
when we first knew.

and the daughters lie awake in their beds,
and smile.

what would you do

if there were, after all, the possibility of unicorns.
would you have a lover if it meant the
unicorn would pass you by, indifferent?
or would you wait for her, and, waiting, could you
masturbate, say, or smoke dope?—what
are the demands of unicorns?
or would you say, hey listen, the unicorn's
crazy; try telling her what it's like: the smell,
for instance, of a man on your hands.
would you shrug, ignore the unicorn
(and be forever virgin in this way:
never to know the touch of the unicorn's face?)
or finding the unicorn, would you
sit there, stroking her head and thinking
how silly it was, like a lapdog, or a kitten;
sigh for lost nights, wait for the unicorn to leave;
and find a man to fill your body

or would it be
a thing so full
that never again would you
think
of men, or books, or things to wear;
that nothing would be worth knowing
except that once,
briefly and forever,
there passed on your hand
the silver breath of a unicorn.

daphne

once, i might have dreamed of this
to be loved by a god
to run together through green places
and the glint of sun-gold hair,
to make love in the arms of forests.
once, in a time of softness, i might have dreamed of you.
now
i have run too often past the cold perimeters of dreams:
now, at the sight of you,
my body grows rigid and harsh,
locks into itself;
i forget how to breathe.
go away, go back where you came from,
leave me alone.
only with you gone
can i turn to flesh again,
can i grow my body back.

medusa

listen i'm telling you it's
every bit as ugly as you think it is
ive seen it ive stared at it, it
tears your stomach out you
scream you claw the air the pain
holds on, holds on, listen
youre not imagining too much youre
not imagining anything, believe me it
burns your face off with its smile
you scream believe me you
scream you run you cry
but the legends are wrong.

it is those who do not look
who turn to stone.

psyche

e elopement, of course, was the scandal of the year.
ll no one (they said) knew anything about him.
ll yes, he came from a
od family, but still
ey said).
r parents were heartbroken.
r older sister was horrified, and very curious.
r younger sister
no lived in new york and was a hippy & was rumored to be a lesbian
d it was silly.
r christsake, psyche,
e said you dont know what the dude looks like.
nean, he might have goddam leprosy he might
ok like a lizard.
nean you dont want to be making it with a goddam lizard do you?
yche giggled.
r mother cried.
r older sister said there was
thing could be done about it.
r younger sister
ve her a lantern she picked up in a head shop in mexico.
psyche took the lantern & walked up the hill to
here she lived with her husband & next day walked down again &
oved into a house alone.
r parents were shocked & left town with her older sister.
r younger sister the hippy asked what did he look like but
yche shook her head.
ter a while everyone got bored & stopped talking about it.
psyche lives in her house & is pleasant & discreet & smiles at the neighbors.
e never talks about her husband:
vertheless it is noticed that she
ways keeps her lights on,
rarely entertains
ntlemen.

the furies

Your world is ripe with us: we're everywhere.
Each breath you breathe inhales our vision's end
Nothing remains unchanged. In its most hidden lair
Your world is ripe with us. We're everywhere
You are. We frame your laughter and despair.
We are your no-man's-land. Sweet sister, friend,
Your world is ripe with us. We're everywhere:
Each breath you breathe inhales our vision's end.

visions
(for Joan)

i—Gorgon

i will grow snakes in my hair;
when you touch my face they will leap at you.
i will grow poison in my breath;
when you come near me they will suffocate you.
i will grow a body so ugly
at the sight of it you will turn to stone, and die.
and i will flee to the place where the gorgons live,
and i will touch the snakes in my sisters' hair:
and the snakes will be rainbows.

ii—The Gray Women
(for SW)

because it is we who see the way,
and only together/ this vision, holy as the moon,
holy as the silent twilight that sustains us/
this vision we hold in our hands
grows in its passage/ contains its muted light/
trembles with the wonder of itself.
sister do not leave.

alone we are blind/
the enemy seizes the vision,
dulls it, fills it with shadow.
sister give me your light; take mine.
alone, we see with their eyes/
we are less than blind.
stay with me.
this is no small thing we hold in our hands,
and it is everything we have.

FALLING OFF THE ROOF

poem for my twentyfifth birthday

this is what it was when i was a kid.
margarine.
fat margarine in cellophane,
white, with a wonderful red spot like a dime, or a chicken pock.
& my job was,
to squeeze the dot till it spread around & got bigger & lighter
& to squeeze the whole fat cellophane package
for ten minutes or another long bunch of time while my
mother cooked or cleaned the oven & our gal sunday was
locked in a cave, with a funny voice
till there was no red spot in the margarine, it was all fat
                                        & yellow & warm
& i kept on squeezing till my mother who was very big took it
                                        away from me & next
week there was another one.
one time there wasnt any more fat margarine, just
little sticks with no red spot & hard & my
mother thought it was great but i was mad as hell
& that was the end of the squeezing & the fat squishy margarine
                                        & our gal sunday
& thats how i started getting twentyfive in the first place.

melmac dishes and linoleum rugs

You do not find them in homes with plastic slipcovers
and knitted dolls on rolls of toilet paper.
They live
on the edges of not-quite-poverty,
on rundown blocks in queens, the bronx,
washington heights, somerville,
with frayed lawns and furniture born shabby—
small homes with mortgages that live forever.
They are cheap to buy, and will not be replaced
next year, or later. They have no style,
and their style does not change.
They cannot be destroyed by tracked-in dirt,
or children's clumsiness,
or the quiet shatterings of despair.
On the rugs are pictures of rugs,
as though they could erase their threadbare truth
with imitations of their betters.
The dishes are garish and direct.

I have a love for these things: they have been with me
through all the places of my life—
sturdy and ugly,
vulgar as survival.

bodies
(July 1971)

i

your
body no longer there i
feel not
comfortable wearing mine
so find myself sleeping
nightgowned
like keeping a door locked
because theres nothing outside

ii

today the astronauts returned dead
life gone from their bodies
coolly, without the
usual explanations.
in worlds outside the world
death has its own set of rules:
delivers, unharmed,
unbloodied, a body
perfect, except
that life's walked out, and hasnt left a note.

summary

there were little hairs on his back,
a suntan line,
a mole.
you watched them like an old film on television
one night when there was nothing better to do.
you remember them now.
you always will.
you remember all the places
you have visited alone.

poem

i

you handled him
as if he were a rosary,
your mind drifting,
your fingers
doing what they were taught to do.

ii

oh, that was a fine one.
you gasped, you moaned, you
bit your lip, your
muscle spasmed, your nipples
hardened and went red;
doctor ruben would approve of it,
beethoven would write a symphony to it.
you waited patiently
for your body to finish its business,
thinking of sleep,
dreaming of solitude.

women who love men

women who love men
enjoy the company of gay men.
if there is not fulfillment here, there is
a space for the closing of eyes.

women who love men
rest their heads in the laps of unicorns.

women who love men
stare through glass walls
at the miracle of woman and woman,
the richness of possiblility
they long
for that most sensible of longings,
and touch their bodies
only in themselves.

women who love men
live in gray rooms above bars,
with no hot water,
and the night filled with alien sounds.

women who love men
lust after secrecy,
hide behind bathroom doors
to smile at the blood weaving down their legs,
the smell of their cunts on their hands.

women who love men
know diogenes was a woman,
they shelter her sad little lamp,
letting themselves quiver at the sight of shadows
they know are shadows.

women who love men
learn to love solitude more.

the fear

because you have spoken of what has happened
it has not happened.
it is a book you've read, a film you saw;
less.
you run down streets, screaming;
the streets erase themselves behind you.

all night you lie awake,
reading your passport to find out where you've been.

take one or two every three hours, as needed

i

the shoemaker's wife goes barefoot,
& the butcher's son's gone vegetarian:
the psychiatrist's daughter
begs the moon for madness.

we all ask for too much these days: this is not my
peculiarity.

ii

shoemaker. see also, *cobbler*.

iii

do not despise the strength of madwomen
vomiting the husks of swallowed moonbeams,
or the power of naked emperors.

borrower

always there,
the need, terrible as sin,
to wear someone else's life like a
hat that doesnt quite fit but
everyone knows is lovely.
and there they always are, waiting to pat you on the head,
or give you a candy apple.
what a good girl you are, now you're one of us.
shall i wear a wig made from your hair, sleep
with your lovers?
give me a list of your vocabulary, tell me
how you won the spelling bee.
everything you say is right, whoever you are.
the love of robots pulls at me like a drug. this
is what i'll be when i grow up.

this place has no end, this labyrinth of magnets.
i will not borrow my life.
if the blood runs from my body in terror, let it.
it will be my blood flowing, my
life dying.

summer

the day is warm the
curtains swell with breezes
you dance to the wonder of your body
the roundness of breasts amazes you
the richness of skin the
deep blue of veins you are
beautiful as the sky, and the breeze knows it
you dance into the sunlight where
three men tell you your tits are bouncing and
one man asks would you like to suck his cock

you remember that little girls draw houses

walls

it took me so long to cherish my perimeters.

hating myself, i crammed my spaces with lovers,
with friends, with telephones,
violating myself like a thousand rapists until,
half crazy and wanting to die
i vomited them all up, cleaned myself out, and began to heal.
i have learned to be my own pygmalion,
building a self from the raw materials of my needs.
my world is rooted in boundaries now,
in doors that are closed and entered by invitation only.
solitude is my core, and work.
my walls are sanity, and you
are trying to break them down.

my sister,
your needs invade me as no man ever has.
(there is no invasion in fucking--
the sweet sharing of what is irrevocably separate.
the cock swells upward to meet the cunt,
the cunt opens its walls to surround the cock;
there is the brief, explosive dance of unity and then
the cunt closes its walls, the cock retreats into itself,
warmly and gently, solitude returns.)

with us there is neither lust nor harmony,
only a door wedged open
and blocking both solitude and connection.
find what you want with others;
i need to be alone, to share the spaces of my intimacy
with comrades who speak my language because it is their own.

straight poem

it isnt easy
to throw away the alphabet
no matter what obscenities they scribble on subway walls.
i have not forgotten you.
i have not stopped loving you, or remembering i love you.
listen,
if i never touch you again,
i will always be touching your absence.
did you think i had forgotten that?

i want it easier than this.
i want to open a door and walk into a room
filled with everything:
books and desks and rugs and furry teddy bears
and a bed with a man on it, waiting for me, loving me.
you know the room—
the one with the trap door under the mirror.
the one with the bear trap hidden in the
arms of the papier mâché lover.
you walk over to him. you lean on him, you say,
hold me,
and he does, oh he does...
you gnaw free through your own bones,
over and over,
you grow weak, waiting to see if the pieces grow back.

do i have to keep on searching you, like a tv cop,
looking for weapons, looking for traps?
i want to touch you softly.
i want to see your eyes.
listen; there is a warmth in the hardnesses of men,
did you think i had forgotten?
and the sweetness in that joining together
like the pieces of some crazy jigsaw puzzle—
did you think i had forgotten that?
i have left you to grow whole again,
i have left you to grow eyes, to invent words.
i am building a place to live,
it is mine; i am whole here,
but lonely—and there is a place for you.

falling off the roof
(for Emily Culpepper)

swollen cotton
drops, blood
swirls in water
red and wet as our mother's first and glorious sin
red
as the glowing skin of the
apple you may not touch
wet as the rich flesh
of the fruit you may not taste
red & wet & i have finally
plunged my hand into my bloody cunt
licked my fingertips and
smeared my face with blood with
war
paint. . .

when i learn to love my blood,
the revolution's begun

abraham lincoln and the pig

i

when i was very young my father told me about abraham lincoln and the pig. the story is this: abraham lincoln & his friend rode in a carriage on a cold & rainy night & they spoke about altruism. there is no such thing said abraham lincoln; nonsense said his friend. just then they heard terrible screams & abraham lincoln looked out the window & saw a pig caught in the mud under a fence, squealing. and abraham lincoln

jumped out of the carriage & into the cold rainy night & knelt in the mud next to the pig & got the pig out from under the fence & the pig ran off and abraham lincoln returned wet & filthy to the carriage. you see said his friend triumphantly that was altruism. and abraham lincoln said no it wasnt i didnt want to waste time worrying about the pig. my father

told me this story when i was very young & since then ive carried it with me, like an amulet against despair. sometimes, amulets dont work.

ii

i could never renounce my father's name
as so many of my people have.
i am too much his child:
my face is his, my laughter—
even my dreams are his dreams, grown larger.
my roots are in his anger.

listen sisters,
listen comrades,
i'm not consorting with the enemy;
i havent consorted in months.
some of my friends think this is very brave. some
think it is very cowardly. i think it
is so much of both that it cancels itself out—
six of one and half a dozen.
my eyes are brown, like my father's.
i shield them behind my glasses,
and sometimes see more than i want to.

iii

sometimes more than anything else, i want to be
a straight   white   man   —
to take a leave of absence from the revolution, wish it luck, promise to
give it a call.
sometimes i hate the men i love
for walking down the street in safety.
sometimes i smile at the men i hate
because it is safer to be on their side.

43

one day when my brother keith was nineteen & the war was still news pop went to the barbershop & the men were talking about draftdodgers & they said that they'd had to fight & by god their sons would & pop walked out & came home & cried & kept saying over & over they'd kill their own sons. then keith got drafted & pop wanted him to go to canada. he went to vietnam instead & for two years we didnt know if he'd died or killed anyone. then he came back & got married & had a daughter. sometimes, when i think of the revolution, i think of my niece & her daughters & all our granddaughters. sometimes it feels warm & good, thinking of them.

but sometimes when im very very tired & nothing moves, i understand those men in the barbershop & i hate my great granddaughters because im living this damned revolution & wont see the end of it & it'll all go to them & what have they done to deserve it? & then i think, i havent changed the world & im not even a nice person anymore. & sometimes i wonder if i was ever really very nice.

sometimes i get to feeling the revolution doesnt love me.
sometimes i think it
kisses me on the cheek & then sneaks out with
some nineteen year old with teased hair & too much makeup.
then i get drunk & throw things & yell,
ive given you the best years of my life.
& the revolution just sits there & doesnt say a thing.

papa,
tell me about abraham lincoln & the pig.
i need to cry, i cant cry anymore.
let me be little & weak while you tell me how
big & strong i am.
when i was little you told me about the lynchings,
you told me about the gas chambers.
you even told me about the indians.
but you didnt tell me about my people,
you didnt tell me the revolution was my job.
sometimes i dont know anything. sometimes
i dont want to know.
papa, tell me about abraham lincoln & the pig.
tell me that the revolution is in my breasts & in my blood.
papa, tell me about the pig. tell me
how to cry again.

and tell me i can do it.

STRATEGIES

hitchhiking

it's not just rapists & killers—
the fear of ending up a
graduation photo in the daily news—
that keeps me from traveling this way,
standing on a road in
comfortable old clothes, and a sign telling where im going—
it's an older fear,
of something owed & not paid;
something that goes on staying with you,
like a ring on a swollen finger.
it's no more blessed to give than to receive;
only easier.
i give my dollars to the faceless driver;
and stay where i am.

i'm

going to read a book or
pick my nose or get married.
i'm going to buy a jar of organic peanut butter.
i'm going to join the revolution & bomb
the pentagon or howard johnsons or the ladies room at city center.
i'm going to knit a yellow douche bag.
i'm going to step on a fat spider or
dip my friend's toothbrush in vinegar.
i'm going to run home,
curl my legs around a dream,
open the box where i hide my silences,
& shut the whole goddam world up for a whole bunch of years.

meaning i

dont know what it is but there
it is
meaning
it's out to get me never you
mind
turning corners slyly are
they following me or will it be at
night softsleeping while they
wait on the fire escape
(it's no city for a young girl, and alone)
or it's you maybe, making up words drink-
ing tea with me why
not?
or my
body, growing strange terrible things
hidden in warm funguses growing growing waiting to
explode the
body's no friend, never
mind the softness of hair on naked shoulder thin-
ness of waist fingertips
against the stubble of new-shaven leg.
it is not to be trusted,
worms live in it and it caresses them
(come with me i will
teach you fears you never dreamed of

i know who i am: sleeping
beauty, with insomnia.
trapped in a brambled world, no company but
snoring statues christ!
the snoring, a hundred years of it!
and the waiting. waiting, waiting a
century for that great something, magic! thats what i
have to wait for thats the rule zap!
the brambles will open & in comes the golden prince
& knowing o yes i know he'll have buck teeth or bad
breath or a small cock
theres no way out

(did i
mention i was a woman? this is
essential to the story. the story i'm
telling. but maybe you guessed, youre very
clever i can tell, farsighted, perceptive,
you tell me how to get out of here.
you promised you would. you remember when.
a thousand years ago, before you were born.
a gleam in your granddaddy's eye.
adam was the first woman, a
chunk of his body torn out to start a world.
but eve discovered joy,
and it was her kind they punished

who is that following me? do you know
him, where does he live, whats his address,
what does he want me for?
will i like him, do you think?

jane, you left the water running
(May, 1970—for Jane Alpert)

this is the rule:
    it is better to kill roaches than kittens,
    but better to kill kittens than people.
i remember this, drowning a roach in the bathroom sink,
my kitten watching, round-eyed and unconcerned.
we measure agony to the scale of our height,
and kill each other in droves.
it's night, i can't sleep, counting
construction workers.
insomnia's too honest to be noble.
bobby seale, lost in prison, fred hampton,
dead in bed (we
call them blacks instead of niggers, & if you kill one you get
demoted),
mostly it's the six kids who
happened to be there, and died,
and what im frightened of is,
it isnt even safe to be white anymore

they arent dreams, these images
shooting at my bed like bullets:
dead women, lost women, frightened women,
black women running through fire,
it doesnt matter if you lock the door,
the sky really is falling (

        UPI—A large chunk of sky dislodged today, and
        fell to earth, killing thousands and completely
        destroying the town of Flushing, N.Y. One of the
        few survivors, pretty, miniskirted Kathleen
        Donovan, reported hysterically that the sky was
        made of fire. These reports proved inaccurate;
        a small segment of sun had apparently fallen with
        the sky, burning several people to death. Most of
        the victims, however, were smothered by blue mist.
        Miss Donovan, 19, was taken to Queens General
        Hospital, along with other survivors, and treated
        for shock and second degree burns.

to turn, where?
my lover sleeps soundly, wrapped in his nightmare,
and theres no man
can answer this cry.
a chunks gone from the sky, i
can't fix it. o my god i am.
heartily.
for killing a roach, sorry.
i always hold my ears when i kill them,
hiding from their screams.
my friend says, they dont scream, so i hold my ears
against their silence.

no screams. or laughter. or weeping.
when we give the earth back to them, they will take it silently.
to crawl silently, along a silent earth.
eating dust.
would be enough, if we could earn it.

jane, you left the water running;
the house is flooded, and the street, the world.
jane, doing what must be done,
forgive me, huddled in my blanket,
afraid of guns, and bombs, and tall men.
revolution is a gift like poetry,
only it matters.
jane, the water's running, the world's an ocean & the swordfish shall
inherit the earth.
tumbling from the backs of glistening dolphins,
we fall, screaming and whimpering, into our sea
. . . and finally sleep
sleep as soft as death
releasing me
to gentler nightmares . . .

april 29, 1975 – the surrender of saigon

i would dance in the streets but my legs have turned to steel
i would sing in triumph but my throat is made of fire
i would celebrate the living but the dead rebuke me

for ten years their deaths have framed our lives
for ten years we have watched them die each night
and marched and chanted   *hey hey LBJ*
                                           how many kids did you kill
                                           today?
till the sound of our voices sickened us
& still they burned & bled & starved & still
the white and gloating faces told us nightly that
the enemy was dying the
enemy was killing our people the enemy was
seizing the enemy's land
& still we marched & chanted   *Ho Ho Ho Chi Minh*
                                      NLF is gonna win

                        old poet old father
they have marched into that final city without you
who should have lived for this
who should have laughed at the back of fleeing invincibility . . .
                        old poet it is not over.
they have tucked away their armies, the
awkward intermediaries of death,
but the blood of chile drowns my laughter,
and a thousand other horrors
the women die the men die the
scorekeepers ignore them but their screams
reach me and i do not sleep.
    old father rejoice, if there is joy for the dead,
walk silent through the city that wears your name,
your triumph
i would rejoice with you i would sing
i would dance in the streets

but the streets are flooded with death

the sins of the fathers
(for Kathy Power)

are visited on the daughters.
alien in the fatherland
you fought with the weapons of their ignorance.
now, they are tracking you down.
kathy,
may we never meet,
may i never have the chance to betray you,
may my love follow you
like the dream of a sleeping goddess
awakening, finally, in the blood of her daughters,
and leading us all
home at last.

the year of the woman
(for Joan Little, Dr. Edelin, and all the others)

i

in the Year of the Woman
you seal us in closed walls
you tear into our bodies
and you graciously call us *ms.*
youve come a long way baby and baby it
is ready or not nice girls do and
good girls dont and if you do why you
can just pay for your fun
and,
if she wasnt looking for it
what was she doing in a place like that.
how many of us will die in the year of the woman?
how many sealed-off wombs?
how many telephone calls from how many laughing rapists?
how many times will our blood be torn from us, this year?

we never asked you for a Year,
wrapped up in pink ribbons and presented with a kiss.
a Year is not what we want.
we want our bodies, we want our souls.
we want our lives.
and we know what it is we're getting.

they told me it was the year of the woman so i
asked them, what woman?

you know, they said—*the* woman.
i said, joan little? they said, no.
i said, inez garcia? they said, no.
i said, jackie onassis? i was getting warm.
but no, they said. no, none of them.
they wouldnt give me a name,
so ive been trying to track her down—
i havent found her yet, but ive got some clues.
the woman is not poor.
she is married with two children.
she does not use contraceptives and does not believe in abortion.
she never says no to her husband.
she will never have more than two children.
she is, of course, a virgin.
her husband washes the dishes and is proud of her career,
which makes her a better mother.
she is not black.
she does not go out alone at night.
her hair is blond, but not too blond,
because that would be asking for it.
she is not a lesbian.
she is 22, and planning to stay that way.
she is a very interesting woman.
maybe i'll get to meet her someday.

do you find this amusing? do you approve of me?
now theres a girl with a sense of humor,
theres a girl who can laugh at herself.
do you really think im laughing?
im not laughing
joan isnt laughing.
inez isnt laughing.
the woman in the hospital isnt laughing.
even the blond virgin with two kids and the rich husband isnt laughing.
she finally understands that you're planning to kill her.
your speeches change nothing, the big hand for the little lady changes noth
it is the year of the woman,
and you smile at us across the bodies of our dead.

next year, you tell us, will be even better.

the campaign

to begin with
we will redefine 7 o'clock.
it will no longer be an hour.
it will be a color,
a new kind of hat,
a thing to give your children when they have behaved
exceptionally well.
you will no longer get up at 7 o'clock,
or have dinner at 7 o'clock,
or meet your lover at 7 o'clock.
you will not leave your lover at 7 o'clock
to return to your wife and kids.
you will not take your pill at 7 o'clock.
you will not lie in stirrups at 7 o'clock
waiting for the doctor to arrive.
it will no longer be
a possibility.

you are angry with me.
you tell me this is trivial, i am
wasting the revolution's time.
i tell you you're wrong.
i tell you it is a beginning—
a good beginning, a fine beginning.
it is the best beginning we have ever had.